C000274213

A CENTURY IN PHOTOGRAPHS

Published jointly by
West Sussex Federation of Women's Institutes
and Countryside Books

COUNTRYSIDE BOOKS
3 Catherine Road
Newbury, Berkshire

ISBN 1 85306 483 1

FRONT COVER PHOTOGRAPH OF AN EARLY
MOTORBIKE AND SIDECAR AT EAST DEAN SUPPLED BY
ANNE SERRAILLIER – SINGLETON & EAST DEAN WI

BACK COVER PHOTOGRAPH SHOWING BOGNOR REGIS IN 1921
SUPPLIED BY SYLVIA ENDACOTT

Designed by Graham Whiteman

Produced through MRM Associates Ltd., Reading

Printed by Woolough Bookbinding Ltd., Irthlingborough

CONTENTS

Land girls at Cowdray ruins, Midhurst in 1943. (WSFWI)

FOREWORD

Our book, *West Sussex Within Living Memory*, was a great success so it seemed fitting we should welcome the suggestion of a pictorial record of the 20th century in this green and pleasant county. The photographs depict happenings in the life of people in West Sussex through the years and show how beautiful our countryside is, from the Downs to the Weald and the coast.

Our grateful thanks go to all those who lent photographs and especially to Mrs Betty Pennicott, our co-ordinator, who accomplished her task with enthusiasm and attention to detail.

We hope this book will arouse many happy memories and give a true picture of the changes that have taken place in our community.

Gillian Yarham
County Chairman

ACKNOWLEDGEMENTS

When agreeing to be co-ordinator for this project I had no idea what it involved — which was just as well! It's been an interesting exercise and I've learned a lot more about the county of my birth.

My grateful thanks to all members who responded by sending in photographs and especially Sylvia Endacott who has allowed access to her private collection — also the staff of Countryside Books for their help and encouragement.

Betty Pennicott
Hunston WI

INTO THE 20TH CENTURY

~

(1900 – 1919)

With the death of Queen Victoria in 1901, the Edwardian age was born and the Coronation of King Edward VII was celebrated in every town and village in West Sussex. The Motor Car Act of 1904 came into force with a speed limit of 20 mph. The County Council resolved that it was desirable to register motor vehicles because it was important to be able to identify who speeded. As a result of the Act, 91 cars and 107 motor cycles were registered. A bridge was built over the river Arun at Littlehampton to cope with the new vehicles.

Roads were in many places still little better than cart tracks, dusty in summer and muddy in winter. Cars were for the wealthy, ordinary people walked or used horse-drawn vehicles or bicycles to get about. The carrier's cart might be the only link between market towns and outlying villages. Canals carried heavy goods to London.

It was a time of great contrast in the lives of rich and poor, yet all shared the lack of 'mod cons'. Water came from the well, pump or spring and bath night for most families meant a tin bath in front of the fire in the kitchen. Light in the home came from oil lamps or candles, or from fragile gas lights. The blackleaded range or the open fire provided heat and cooking facilities. Food was simple and usually home-grown and home-cooked. There was none of the choice available to later generations.

Horses were used on the land and for transport, and work on the land was labour intensive and traditional. Oxen were still used for ploughing on the Downs, being more sure-footed than horses on the sloping fields. The only sound to be heard on the Downs was that of the sheep bells. Wheelwrights and blacksmiths were amongst the 'aristocracy' of the village, their work essential for all. A good harvest could still mean the difference between comfort and hardship, and haymaking and harvest time brought whole communities out into the fields, young and old alike.

Where there was a 'big house' with a local squire, village life was structured. The vicar was very involved in the lives of his parishioners, particularly where there was a church school. Attendance at church or chapel on Sunday, and Sunday school for the children, was part of life. The Sunday school outing was eagerly awaited, as it was often the only time they were taken on a trip out of the village.

Seaside resorts were beginning to prosper as the railways made them more accessible. Strolling on the 'Prom' at Bognor, donkey rides, Punch and Judy and horse-drawn bathing huts were all part of a seaside holiday. Even when swimming, though, people remained fully covered and even children had sleeves down to their elbows and costume legs down to their knees.

Sir Weetman Dickinson Pearson (later Viscount Cowdray) bought the Cowdray Estate and restored the picturesque ruins in the park. Cowdray Park would become synonymous with polo as the century went on.

Others came seeking the Sussex air, for example the Bluecoat School founded by

1900 – 1919

Edward VI, which moved from Newgate in London to Christ's Hospital near Horsham in 1902.

In 1914 the men of Sussex joined up in their thousands and marched, singing, away to war. At times during the next terrible years, the guns in France could be clearly heard on the Sussex coast. Some foods became very scarce and money was tight for servicemen's families. On 9th November 1915 a meeting was called at Little Drovers in Singleton under the auspices of the parish council and the War Agricultural Committee, when Mrs Alfred Watt and Mrs Hugh Christie spoke on 'Improvement of the Food Supply and the Study of Home Economics'. As a result, Singleton & East Dean Women's Institute was formed, the first in England. They met in the back room of the Fox at Charlton.

Mr Harry 'Shuffler' Carpenter, postman for West Dean and Chilgrove, c1912. Born and bred in West Dean, he went across to Chilgrove twice a day in all weathers, either on foot or by bike. He was also a pillar of the local church.
(Joyce Stant – East Wittering WI)

INTO THE 20TH CENTURY (1900–1919)

A busy scene outside Chichester station in the early 1900s, perhaps on a race day. Horse-drawn transport reigned supreme. (Anne Serraillier – Singleton & East Dean WI)

The Jennings family leaving the Swan Hotel at Pulborough, bound for Goodwood races in 1900. The family ran the hotel from 1897 to 1938. (Marjorie Jennings – Pulborough Meadows WI)

Bottom A view over Goodwood racecourse c1906, the cabs and conveyances empty and waiting.
(Anne Serraillier – Singleton & East Dean WI)

At Ardingly crossroads in 1914 – it is recalled that the horse in the picture was requisitioned for the war and did not return.
(Rosemary Hodgson – Ardingly WI)

TELEPHONE DISASTER   HAYWARDS HEATH   JAN 8TH 09

THEN & NOW. The Horsham road, near Handcross in 1910 and as it looks today.
(Gladys Toogood – Handcross WI)

Telephone lines brought down on a snowy day in January 1908 at Haywards Heath.
(Joyce Newman – Madehurst WI)

One of the attractions on the seafront at Bognor in 1913 was 'Mr Pashley's Aeroplane'. (Sylvia Endacott)

Motorised transport was beginning to prove its worth – the first journey of the Royal Mail parcel post motor coach from London to Brighton was made on 2nd June 1905. It has stopped here at Friars Oak. (Joyce Newman – Madehurst WI)

Pennicott's shop at Singleton bridge c1911. Village shops were a lifeline for rural communities, making regular deliveries to their customers. Many people relied on them for all their needs.
(Anne Serraillier – Singleton & East Dean WI)

Harnett's butcher's shop in London Road, Bognor. Meat was displayed whole and usually hanging outside the shop, in a manner that would be unthinkable today. Many butchers also ran their own small slaughterhouse and bought animals from local markets. (Sylvia Endacott)

Wingate's Dairy, Aldwick, where they kept their own Alderney cows. The churns are ready on the left for delivery direct to the customers. (Sylvia Endacott)

*Alan Arnold in his oyster
boat off the quay at
Bosham.*
(Angela Bromley Martin
– Bosham WI)

Maids at the Manor House, Bosham in 1904. Going into service was often the only choice of career open to young girls. (Angela Bromley Martin – Bosham WI)

Duke the gardener at the Manor House, Bosham in 1903.
The 'big house' and estate provided employment for both
men and women. (Angela Bromley Martin – Bosham
WI)

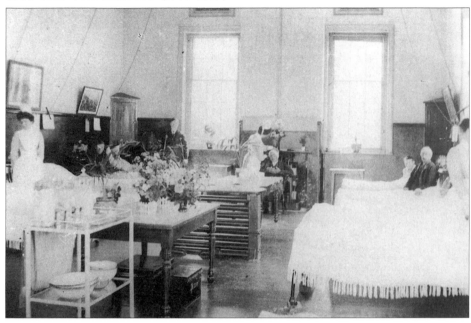

Chichester Infirmary, Dixon Ward, c1913. The nurses were very strictly disciplined and besides their nursing duties had to clean the floors, polish the brass and serve the food. (Anne Serraillier – Singleton & East Dean WI)

In the kitchen of the Holy Cross Convent at Haywards Heath. Cavernous kitchens like these were found in most institutions and big houses, with the blackleaded range the only source of warmth and heat for cookery. (Betty Pennicott – Hunston WI)

Carting the hay at Balcombe in 1903. The sweet scent of hay was one of the pleasures of summertime and haymaking brought the whole family out into the fields. (Balcombe WI)

Harvest time c1912 at Biggs Farm, Cuckfield, using a horse-drawn sail reaper. (Joyce Newman – Madehurst WI)

Horse-ploughing at Balcombe, a skill which was regarded with great pride by the farm workers. (Balcombe WI)

The Young brothers hand-sowing at Biggs Farm, Cuckfield. Broadcasting the seed was still a common practice into this century. (Joyce Newman – Madehurst WI)

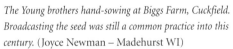

Sheep washing at Lavant c1900. It was a task that always attracted an audience
(Anne Serraillier – Singleton & East Dean WI)

A meeting of Kirdford Calf Club in 1912 – the houses in the background were labourers' cottages, having been in the 1800s the local workhouse (since 1960 they have been a private residence known as Church House). The Calf Club was a forerunner of the Young Farmers' Club.
(Mavis Thompson – Kirdford WI)

Baby Selwyn Lloyd and his nanny Margaret in 1903, with a very ornate baby carriage and an equally ornate bonnet for baby! (Angela Bromley Martin – Bosham WI)

Pupils of Staplefield school in 1910. In some areas, girls continued to wear white pinafores to school into the early 1920s. (Joyce Newman – Madehurst WI)

On the netball courts at Chichester High School for Girls.
No girl would have considered playing sport except in all-
covering clothing.
(Joyce Stant – East Wittering WI)

George 'Grandsire' Arnold and his wife outside their cottage in Bosham. He joined the village choir in 1829, when he was ten years of age, and sang in the choir until he died at the age of 93 in July 1912. He was the longest practising 'choirboy' in England.
(Angela Bromley Martin – Bosham WI)

Climbing Rackman Hill in 1905 – by bike. Notice that the boys, though on holiday, are wearing their school caps.
(Betty Watson – Sullington WI)

The Balcombe tug-of-war team in 1910 – the Heavyweight Champions of Sussex. The tug-of-war took place at the annual Balcombe Flower Show and the men practised for months prior to the big day.
(Balcombe WI)

Ardingly Brass and Reed Prize Band in 1914, after they had won the Southern Counties Challenge Cup. The band survived until the late 1930s and performed at all village functions. They were of a very high standard, taking part in competitions at Tunbridge Wells and at the Crystal Palace, where they won first prize in a national competition. (Rosemary Hodgson – Ardingly WI)

Bosham ladies' cricket team in 1903. (Angela Bromley Martin – Bosham WI)

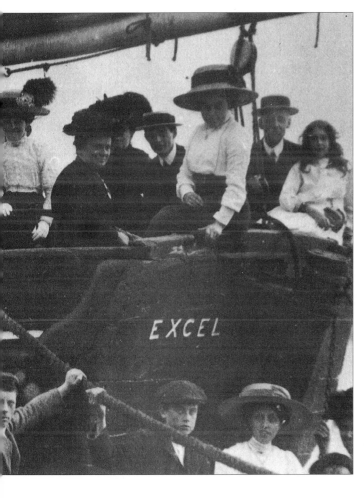

Spectators at Bosham Regatta in 1910, a very popular local event. (Angela Bromley Martin – Bosham WI)

Left Albert Holman, together with his brothers, volunteered for the Royal Sussex Regiment, as did many other men from Ardingly village during the war. He was taken prisoner and spent time as a POW in Germany; his younger brother was decorated. They survived but the village lost 28 men. Every day at noon during the war, the church bell was rung to remind villagers to pray for the servicemen at the Front. (Rosemary Hodgson – Ardingly WI)

The VAD hospital at Balcombe (1914–1919) was equipped with 20 beds. Six hundred cases were treated there – a capitation fee was received for each patient, but all extras were bought with money raised in the village. Dr and Mrs Newton acted as Medical Officer and Matron, and nursing and other staff numbered about 60. All work was voluntary. (Balcombe WI)

Members of Singleton & East Dean Women's Institute planting potatoes on Lambsdown, Singleton in 1916. This was the first English Women's Institute to be founded, in November 1915. Almost immediately members plunged into the war effort, and rented a plot from the local farmer, where they grew vegetables. (Singleton & East Dean WI)

The female station staff at Haywards Heath station in August 1918, outside Station Cottages – three ticket collectors, two porters and, in the light overalls, two clerical staff. The women were taken on only on the understanding that the men had their jobs back when they returned after the war.
(Cilla Bozier – Roffey WI)

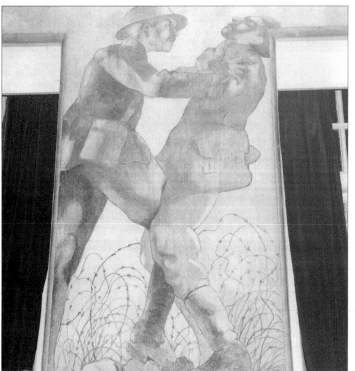

Singleton peace celebrations in 1919, held in the recreation field. Every town and village held teas, sports and other festivities to celebrate the long awaited coming of peace.
(Anne Serraillier – Singleton & East Dean WI)

In 1923 the Victory Hall at Balcombe was built in memory of the men who died during the war, funded by public subscription and by Lady Denman (first chairman of the National Federation of Women's Institutes), who lived in the village and who was closely involved in the planning and decoration of the hall. On the internal walls of the hall were painted unique frescoes depicting scenes of war and peace, executed by Neville Lytton who had himself experienced the horrors of the trenches and of modern warfare.
(Balcombe WI)

31

BETWEEN THE WARS

~

(1920 – 1938)

The Twenties and Thirties were times of great hardship for many families. Returning servicemen had been promised a land fit for heroes, but found instead a shortage of housing and unemployment. The first council houses were built, however, and with their electric lights and airy rooms seemed a taste of paradise for many who had been raised in dark, overcrowded cottages. The General Strike of 1926 and other strikes on the railways and in the mines affected everyone. Coal miners from the depressed areas of England were resettled along the coastal plain of Sussex under the Land Resettlement Scheme.

Women had enjoyed their taste of freedom and independence during the war years but most lost their jobs when the men returned. They got the vote, but women under 30 had to wait until 1928. Opportunities for girls leaving school were few, and employment of any kind usually ended when they got married. There was still a call for servants in upper and middle class homes, and many girls had no choice but to go into service, working long hours for low pay.

Schools had changed little since the turn of the century, though the school leaving age was raised to 14. Further education was only for the better off or the lucky few who got a scholarship. Corporal punishment kept order in the classrooms, and the Attendance Officer kept a close eye on truants. In spite of few facilities, many of the all-age village schools gave their children a good grounding in the three Rs.

Tall sailing ships still came up to Arundel port from Littlehampton with cargoes of timber, coal and salt in the 1930s. On the land, the car was beginning to make its mark on the countryside. The new Norfolk Bridge was built at Shoreham at a cost of £45 million. The first traffic lights were installed in Horsham and at Stopham Bridge. Bypasses were built in several parts of the county, including at Chichester, Coldwaltham, Crawley, Felpham, Findon and Sompting.

Flying became very popular between the wars. In the county, Shoreham Airport was developed and scheduled flights to the Isle of Wight, Deauville and the Channel Islands became a regular feature.

New estates of houses were needed. Franklands Village was built, as was the Aldwick Bay Estate. Rustington airfield became Rustington Sea Estate with bungalows built along the original road surrounding the water tower.

There seemed to be a corner shop on every road in towns, and every village had its general store. Tradesmen came to the house every week to take orders, and deliv-

In Arundel Great Park in 1928, with Hiorne Tower in the background; the children are perched on a German First World War cannon. (Audrey Broad – Southwater Weald WI)

MARY WHEATLAND
BOGNOR'S CELEBRATED BATHING WOMAN.

1920 – 1938

Mary Wheatland was one of Bognor's bathing machine proprietors. This postcard photo was taken in 1906 and on the back the sender has written: 'This old daisy is 72 years of age and has saved in her time over 30 lives…and up to last year used to dive off the end of the pier.' Mary died in 1924.
(Sylvia Endacott)

ered too. Errand boys on bicycles, usually whistling the latest tunes, were to be seen in every town centre. Bakers, butchers, fishmongers, grocers – all had their regular rounds and could be relied on to deliver whatever the weather. Milk was delivered straight from the churn into the customer's jug, though the more hygienic bottles began to be used by some dairies.

King George V convalesced at Craigweil House, and 'Regis' was added to the name of the seaside resort of Bognor – and the King's comment about Bognor, said to have been made on his deathbed, has passed into folklore. The King's Silver Jubilee was celebrated in 1935, and two years later street parties, sports, teas and bonfires greeted the Coronation of King George VI.

Bathing machines on the beach at Bognor Regis in 1921. This set belonged to Mr Jenkins, who used three horses – Beauty, Major and Lion – to pull the machines into the sea. He was in business from the 1890s until he sold up in 1936. (Sylvia Endacott)

A family day out on Bognor beach in 1927. Everyone is
fully clothed, with most of those in the background in hats
and coats – a typical summer's day!
(Joyce Mack – Aldwick West WI)

Goat carts were a popular
attraction with children in
front of Bognor Pier in the
1920s, the Ashton Brothers
being among the owners.
Rides cost 3d.
(Sylvia Endacott)

Left Bognor's West Parade in the late 1930s. A new sea
wall was built here in the 1980s to prevent the annual
flooding of this area. (Sylvia Endacott)

Right High Street, Ardingly in the 1920s. The telegraph and electricity poles have gone now, all underground, but there are street lights, the first having been given by Sir Henry Price to celebrate the Coronation in 1953. The pump house, which supplied families with water, did not disappear until the late 1950s. 'Traffic now is…well, need I say?'
(Rosemary Hodgson – Ardingly WI)

Above *A peaceful scene at Swan Corner, Pulborough in the 1920s, with the Swan Hotel in the background.*
(Betty Watson – Sullington WI)

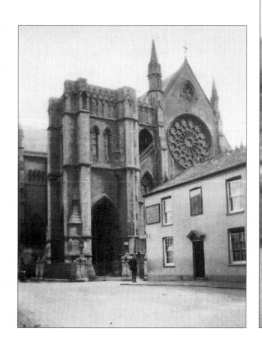

Arundel Cathedral in the 1920s. The scene has hardly changed today, apart from cars on the road.
(Betty Watson – Sullington WI)

ARDINGLY HIGH STREET

The Atora Suet cart delivering at Fernhurst, 1930. This eye-catching pair of oxen were an unusual sight in the village lanes. (Helen Ollin – Fernhurst WI)

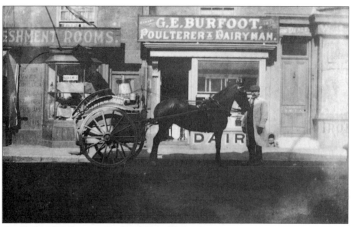

Smith's butcher's shop at West Hoathly in the 1920s. The tradesman's horse and cart or bicycle began to give way to motorised delivery vans by the 1930s. The building is now used as a Roman Catholic chapel and doctor's surgery.
(Pauline Ralph – West Hoathly WI)

Burfoot's milk delivery cart in the 1920s, with the churn and measures ready. The shop was in High Street, Shoreham, opposite the Town Hall.
(June Lewis – Shoreham Greenways WI)

Fernhurst post office in the 1930s, with the Royal Mail van just arrived. In most villages, the post office possessed the only telephone at this time.
(Helen Ollin – Fernhurst WI)

Kirdford Garage and Cycle Shop, 1934, owned by Mr R. Snelling who was also the local postman. At this time bicycles were just as important as cars for most people, particularly for getting to and from work every day.
(Mavis Thompson – Kirdford WI)

Drawing water at Fernhurst in the 1920s. Many country homes continued to rely on wells, pumps or streams into the 1950s. (Helen Ollin – Fernhurst WI)

Left Mr A. Barnard, village policeman at West Hoathly, in 1935. The 'village bobby' was an integral part of rural life. (Pauline Ralph – West Hoathly WI)

A Brownie presenting a bouquet to Queen Mary, when she was staying at Balcombe in April 1927. (Balcombe WI)

At Guide camp in 1928 – the Whitsun weekend at Coates Castle, Fittleworth. Holidays were still something of a rarity for many children and going away to camp was a wonderful adventure. (Barbara Musson – Lurgashall WI)

Taking the new baby for an airing in 1937.
(Betty Pennicott – Hunston WI)

West Hoathly school stoolball team in the 1920s.
(Pauline Ralph – West Hoathly WI)

A Mothers' Union outing at Fernhurst in 1920. Charabancs were enormously popular for group outings, giving a sedate ride in the open air. If it rained the cover at the back could be pulled over. (Edie Lucas – Fernhurst WI)

A charabanc works outing in the early 1920s for Munnions Builders, for whom many Ardingly men worked. The coach probably belonged to Mr Simmonds, who had the first garage in the village. Note the beer or cider jar prominently displayed!
(Rosemary Hodgson – Ardingly WI)

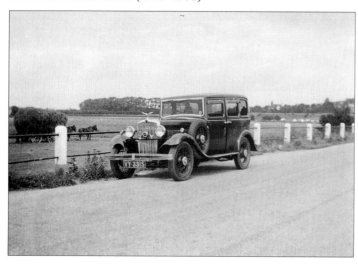

Just south of Houghton Bridge on the B2139. The car is a 1932 Morris Major, bought in Bognor in 1934 for £55. In the background can be seen a horse-drawn hay wagon.
(Betty Watson – Sullington WI)

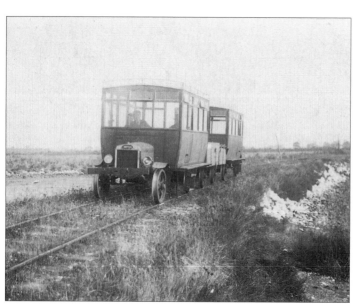

The Selsey tram which ran between Chichester and Selsey, 1935. It was so slow that passengers were able to alight and pick flowers or mushrooms along the way and hop on again. (Dorothy Triggs – Donnington WI)

Harvesting statice at Burfoot Bros' Kingston Nurseries, Shoreham in the 1920s. The flowers were grown on a commercial scale for local suppliers .
(June Lewis – Shoreham Greenways WI)

A milk tanker outside The Creamery, Kirdford in 1927. This was a collection and distribution depot for local farm milk, testing and pasteurising it here before it went up to London in the early afternoon.
(Mavis Thompson – Kirdford WI)

47

Timber felling at Kirdford in 1925 – a very active local industry for almost the whole of the century but now gone. (Mavis Thompson – Kirdford WI)

Charcoal burners at work in the woods around Balcombe in the 1920s, building the kiln in which charcoal would be made. This traditional industry lasted until the 1940s in the area and many local people can recall when men worked and lived in the forest. (Balcombe WI)

Top The Warren, West Dean, where pheasants were reared for shooting, c1921. Estates provided much of the local employment at one time.
(Anne Serraillier – Singleton & East Dean WI)

Someone always has to wash up! In 1927, after an outdoor church luncheon at West Worthing, there were piles of china plates to be washed and wiped.
(Cilla Bozier – Roffey WI)

49

Playing whist in the old vicarage garden (now The Close) at Shoreham by Sea in the 1920s.
(June Lewis – Shoreham Greenways WI)

The Women's Institutes held a 'Century Day' at Wiston Park on 25th June 1930, when members dressed in fashions from past days.
Steyning WI)

*At Bosham Regatta in
1937.*
(Angela Bromley Martin
– Bosham WI)

*A beautifully decorated cart ready for the show, at Manor
Farm, Southwick. From the royal motifs, this may have
been ready for the celebrations for George V's Silver Jubilee
in 1935.* (Joan Cooper –Rustington WI)

BETWEEN THE WARS (1920–1938)

A celebration children's fancy dress parade held on 12th May 1937 for the Coronation of George VI. All over the county there were parties, bonfires and fireworks.
(Audrey Broad – Southwater Weald WI)

THE SECOND WORLD WAR

(1939 – 1945)

War was declared on Sunday, 3rd September 1939, but it was some time before the effects were felt. This was the period of the 'phoney war', but it ended on the beaches at Dunkirk in June 1940. Some of the armada of 'little boats' that went across to France to rescue our army were from ports and harbours in Sussex.

Now invasion seemed a very real possibility and all the war measures so far took on a new significance. The civilian population had never before been so involved in a war. Everyone was urged to do their bit – many joined the Home Guard, the ARP, the Observer Corps, the WVS and all the other organisations that together guarded and gave help to their communities. The Fire Service was nationalised for greater efficiency.

The blackout was rigorously imposed. Car headlights had to be partly shielded so that as little light as possible was cast. Street lamps were unlit, making walking a hazardous business at times. 'Put that light out!' became a familiar cry from the local air raid wardens, keen to prevent even a chink of light escaping to help enemy bombers.

Air raid shelters were built or dug in towns, and Anderson shelters issued for the garden or Morrison shelters for inside the house. Gas masks had been distributed immediately and the fear of a gas attack remained a horrific possibility. Masks had to be carried at all times, even by children.

Over two million evacuees were expected in West Sussex from areas that suffered heavy bombing. Some schools were not big enough to take them, so other buildings were pressed into service, including village halls and even tea rooms. Schoolchildren grew vegetables, gathered blackberries, raised poultry and rabbits, and helped in the collection of waste paper and scrap metal.

Rationing was imposed from the start and every bit of available ground was dug up to plant vegetables. The Women's Land Army filled the shoes of the men called up into the services, and girls from all walks of life learned to plough, milk cows and tend crops. The government emphasised the importance of preserving the fruit harvest and the Women's Institutes answered the call by opening jamming centres in many villages.

Tangmere airfield, built during the First World War, became the home of the Hurricane fighters and during the Battle of Britain dogfights in the sky between British and German pilots were a common sight. In one raid, 14 planes were destroyed on the ground at the airport. From Tangmere, Lysanders carried secret agents into the

In the underground ARP control room at County Hall, Chichester in 1941 – on duty were Mark Hughes, County Treasurer, and Gordon Bearman, County Librarian. (Steyning WI)

Reinforcements for the Normandy Front in 1944 – an LST loaded with equipment including rolls of chestnut fencing for trackways on the beaches. Many were supplied by Fernhurst Chestnut Fencing Co. at Henley Common. (Helen Ollin – Fernhurst WI)

heart of Occupied Europe. There was great activity around Thorney Island too, and other important airfields at Ford, Westhampnett and Shoreham.

Movement along the coast was restricted, and the beaches were out of bounds. In 1944 preparations for D-Day began, with coastal areas used for the embarkation of tanks and military hardware.

VE Day in May 1945 was greeted with celebrations and huge relief. Street parties were held all over the country. It was time at last for the lights to go on and for street names and signposts to reappear. Park flower beds could go back to growing flowers, and it was time too for the long process of clearing mines to begin on the beaches.

THE SECOND WORLD WAR (1939–1945)

Bomb damage to cottages in Ardingly 1940. These houses suffered a direct hit and five adults from two families were killed. The two adjoining houses also had to be demolished. There were searchlights and gun emplacements in the village, as it was a bomber route, and this may explain the attack. Ardingly also survived a landmine and a V1 rocket. Twelve men from the village were killed in the services.
(Rosemary Hodgson – Ardingly WI)

Ardingly Home Guard outside the village hall, 1940, led by officers Arnold and Kier Hett, of Hapstead Hall. 'The members of the Home Guard really did parade with broom handles for drill practice before they were issued with rifles.'
(Rosemary Hodgson – Ardingly WI)

Inspection of the Girls' Training Corps at Arundel Castle cricket ground in 1942. The Corps was formed in the early days of the war to give girls some experience of service life – drilling, aircraft recognition, vehicle maintenance etc.
(Audrey Broad – Southwater Weald WI)

Men and women of the Observer Corps at Fernhurst in 1943. The reports made by the Corps were essential links in the chain of defence against enemy bombing raids.
(Helen Ollin – Fernhurst WI)

Chichester's Civil Defence Corps in 1939.
(Heather Crate – Hunston WI)

The Royal Family travelled the length and breadth of England keeping morale high – Queen Elizabeth was at County Hall, Chichester in 1940. She is pictured here with T. C. Hayward, the Countess of Bessborough and Lord Leconfield.
(Steyning WI)

Threshing at Weyhurst Farm.
(Barbara Musson – Lurgashall WI)

Land girls Barbara Brownslow and Rosemary Horton. The photo was taken just before they went to Portsmouth for a big parade at which they held the banner calling for girls to join the Land Army.
(Rosemary Cundell – Funtington & West Stoke WI)

Left Barbara Musson taking a welcome tea break at Weyhurst Farm in 1944, when soldiers came to help with the haymaking. (Barbara Musson – Lurgashall WI)

Right Mr and Mrs Moller outside their shop and post office at West Dean. The baker, Ern Boxall, made bread and cakes in the old bakehouse at the back. (Anne Serraillier – Singleton & East Dean WI)

Mr Roberts, landlord of the Selsey Arms at West Dean, pulling a pint during the war, with his daughter Mrs Joan Nicklin and 'Snowy' Mechen who worked as a hurdlemaker on the estate. (Anne Serraillier – Singleton & East Dean WI)

Charcoal burners at work in the Charlton Forest during the war, when charcoal was used for industrial purposes and also in the production of gas masks.
(Anne Serraillier – Singleton & East Dean WI)

Rotherfield House was given by Beryl, Lady Cowdray for Midhurst and Easebourne Cottage Hospital in 1939. It was sandbagged against enemy action.
(WSFWI)

Right *Easebourne WI's Produce Show at Midhurst in 1944. People were encouraged to use every scrap of food – 'Waste not, want not, fill your stockpot!' exhorts a notice on the table.*
(WSFWI)

A working party at Easebourne Red Cross depot in 1940, making comforts for the troops.
(WSFWI)

Easebourne children and evacuees having a break from digging their allotment in 1940 – and giving a cheer for the troops!
(WSFWI)

Evacuees from Lambeth taking a keen interest in country life in 1941. This and the other Easebourne photos were taken for publicity purposes, but similar scenes would have been familiar all over the county.
(WSFWI)

*Paper collecting by
Easebourne Scouts in 1941.*
(WSFWI)

*Easebourne Girl Guides'
scrap metal collection in
1941. Children were
encouraged to do their best
to collect salvage – the girls
here are being closely
watched by two local boys!*
(WSFWI)

Two bells were given as a thanksgiving for victory and dedicated on 11th November 1945 at Easebourne church. (WSFWI)

Rabbits were not on ration and a day's rabbiting produced a tasty meal for the pot. Ed Voller presents a couple of rabbits to Annie Lambe of Denyers Cottage, Henley village in 1941. (Helen Ollin – Fernhurst WI)

THE POST-WAR YEARS

(1946 – 1959)

Though the war was over, rationing stayed in force for many years to come. Post-war Britain was a place of austerity and shortages. The bitter winter of 1947 was a hard time for many when coal was still rationed and basic foodstuffs difficult to come by. Bread did not come off ration until the following year, and all food rationing only ended in 1954, after over 14 years.

The Welfare State had been created, with a promise that care would be available 'from the cradle to the grave'. The National Health Service began in 1948, ending the days of the doctor's bill and a reliance on home cures. The railways, mines and other essential industries were nationalised.

Housing was in short supply after the war, so many buildings having been damaged by bombing. Crawley New Town was developed as an overspill for London and from a small village a vast area of houses, shops and open spaces grew. In other areas railway carriages and wooden shacks were gradually replaced with bricks and mortar.

As petrol came off ration, the dream of owning one's own car took hold. More widely available than ever before, and becoming more affordable, cars became part of the family. Streets built in the days of horses and carts now had to cope with the motor vehicle and concerns were soon being voiced about the effects. The first motorway was opened in 1959.

A great flying tradition lived on at Tangmere. In 1953 Neville Duke flew from the airfield and broke the world air speed record at 727 mph in a Hawker Hunter jet fighter.

British Rail closed down the East Grinstead to Lewes line, but thanks to the enthusiasm of a dedicated band of railway buffs part of it eventually reopened – as the much-loved Bluebell Railway.

Despite hardships at home, international concerns now touched everyone. The Freedom From Hunger Campaign was launched, and the plight of starving thousands in war-shattered Europe moved people to give their wholehearted support. The 'Ban The Bomb' movement, too, gathered followers, particularly from amongst the young.

Young people were finding their voice as never before, and their music and dress were changing, to the bafflement of their elders. Further education was open to those who just a decade before would have left school at 14 and gone straight into work.

The Festival of Britain in 1951 was a celebration of life then and in the future. The news of the death the following year of King George VI was received with great sorrow by the nation, who remembered the morale-boosting efforts of the Royal Family during the war. The accession of his daughter as Queen Elizabeth II was, however,

Hay-making time at Parletts Farm, Madehurst in 1956, building the ricks by hand. (Joyce Newman – Madehurst WI)

1946 – 1959

Nurse Selina Harding retired as Singleton's District Nurse in 1956, her service going back as far as 1919. She was the first district nurse to be awarded the MBE.

(Anne Serraillier – Singleton & East Dean WI)

greeted as the dawning of a new Elizabethan Age. Her Coronation in June 1953 was a great occasion, the day enhanced by the news that Sir Edmund Hillary and Sherpa Tenzing had climbed Mount Everest. Many people watched the coronation ceremony on television, their first glimpse of 'the box'. Its lure proved so strong that before the end of the decade nearly two thirds of all households had their own set.

Above A visit on 30th May 1946 by Queen Elizabeth to the King Edward VII Sanatorium at Midhurst. The Royal Family had earned the country's love and respect for their work and support during the war, and it was always a delight to see Queen Elizabeth on her visits to the county. (WSFWI)

First class polo has become synonymous with Cowdray Park and it was not long after the war that the game was being played here again. The match in progress was in 1947, and (above) the young Queen Elizabeth II is shown presenting the cup in 1952. (Evelyn Drew – Lindfield WI; WSFWI)

Above Land girls working
at the Plant Protection
Research Station at
Fernhurst in 1947, where
crops were grown for
research into pesticides etc.
The Women's Land Army
was not disbanded until
1950, there still being such
a demand for labour on the
land in the post-war years
when many foods
remained under ration.
(Muriel Bushby –
Sidlesham WI)

The popular actor Jack
Warner opening a Land
Army rally at Wiston in
1946.
(Muriel Bushby –
Sidlesham WI)

Lady Denman at a Land Army party at Northlands Hostel, Chichester in May 1946.
(Muriel Bushby – Sidlesham WI)

North Lodge, Northgate, Chichester in 1949, new headquarters of the West Sussex Federation of Women's Institutes.
(WSFWI)

Above *Christmas Day at Southlands Hospital, Shoreham in 1947. Times were still hard after the war but efforts were made by everyone to relieve the spartan atmosphere.* (Betty Pennicott – Hunston WI)

Quiet times at the Three Horseshoes pub at Lickfold in 1948. This later became the Lickfold Inn and is now being converted into a restaurant. (Betty Redding – Lurgashall WI)

Apple grading and sorting at Kirdford Growers in 1949. This co-operative of local farmers who combined for the sale and distribution of their fruit was started in 1931. Fruit farming was once a thriving local industry, but in the 1990s orchards were grubbed up, and imported fruit is now stored at the Packhouse to make use of its capacity.
(Daphne Bryder – Kirdford WI)

Combine harvesters in the fields at Findon in 1950, a sign of things to come as work on the land became ever more mechanised.
(Muriel Bushby – Sidlesham WI)

The railway from East Grinstead to Lewes, dating from 1882, was closed in 1957 but later reopened as the Bluebell Railway. The picture shows Sharpthorne Tunnel at West Hoathly, with the now-gone passenger bridge and station house. (Pauline Ralph – West Hoathly WI)

The May Queen procession at Fernhurst in 1950. (Helen Ollin – Fernhurst WI)

A scene to bring back memories – round the campfire with the 1st Albourne Brownie pack (formed in 1954) picnicking on Wolstonbury on Ascension Day 1958.
(Albourne WI)

A spring scene, boys playing out in the fields near the Midhurst-Chichester road in the 1950s.
(Anne Serraillier – Singleton & East Dean WI)

Camping became very popular after the war, and caravanning even more so as car ownership spread. This was the Walnut Tree Camping Site at West Wittering in the 1950s.
(Dorothy Downe – East Wittering WI)

THE SIXTIES AND SEVENTIES

(1960 – 1979)

As the Sixties began, a farmer ploughing his field north of Fishbourne discovered pottery shards that proved to be from the largest Roman palace yet found in Britain. The Weald and Downland Open Air Museum opened at Singleton with the aim of preserving traditional 'vernacular' architecture that would otherwise be destroyed. Old buildings were disappearing at an alarming rate as development and modernisation took place. Luckily, there were those who protected the past, because these were the Swinging Sixties, when youth culture took hold.

Anything seemed possible, when man walked on the moon in 1969 and Concorde flew its maiden supersonic flight. Yet much that was valuable from the past was swept away, leaving some towns with a blight of ring roads, draughty shopping centres and tall concrete blocks of flats and offices.

Beeching's 'axe' fell on branch railway lines and cut a vital link between town and village. Later some of these lines were converted to footpaths, or brought into farming use.

Woods Mill at Small Dole opened as the Field Centre for the Sussex Naturalists' Trust (later changed to the Sussex Trust for Nature Conservation). Nature reserves were opened at Kingley Vale, Pagham Harbour and other smaller sites. In 1964 Chichester Harbour was declared an Area of Outstanding Natural Beauty, and this once working harbour has now become almost entirely a leisure facility. Arundel Wildfowl Trust opened a reserve by Arundel Castle and many species of birds were attracted to the lakes.

The arts were not forgotten. Chichester Festival Theatre was opened, with Sir Laurence Olivier as its first Artistic Director.

The period ended with the Women's Institutes celebrating their Diamond Jubilee. Bramber Beeches was established at Longburrow, Church Farm, Coombes, thanks to the generosity of keen conservationist Dick Passmore. Over 600 trees, including pine, field maple, sycamore, Norway maple, Italian elder and Austrian pine, were planted. As the County Chairman ceremonially dug in a tree, the stalwart members who had gathered in driving rain and gale force winds gave an impromptu rendering of *Jerusalem*!

Despite growing interest in the environment, this was now a consumer society. Most homes could boast a refrigerator, washing machine, television set, private telephone – all things few could have hoped to buy just a decade before.

Traffic was an increasing concern, particularly along the coast where the seaside resorts attracted ever growing numbers of holidaymakers. Freight was also being carried by road now, where once it

Mr Ron Snelling on his last day as Kirdford's village postman, at the age of 90 in 1978. (Mavis Thompson – Kirdford WI)

1960 – 1979

The West Sussex Federation celebrated the Diamond Jubilee of the WI movement at Arundel. Their Highnesses Prince Georg and Princess Anne of Denmark are pictured with nine year old Catherine Phillips, Lady Shakerley, County Chairman, and Joan Lance, Vice Chairman. (WSFWI)

would have been transported by train, and larger and heavier lorries were the result.

In 1974 local government reorganisation resulted in an altering of the boundaries between East and West Sussex. Gatwick Airport 'changed sides' – first licensed in 1930 as a private airstrip it became the second London airport, bringing much employment and prosperity to the area.

THE SIXTIES AND SEVENTIES (1960–1979)

THEN & NOW. The stores and post office at Upper Pendent, West Hoathly in 1914 and the 1960s. The side shop was taken down in the 1950s, and the 17th century timber-framed house and shop became an antiques shop in the 1970s before closing in 1990. (Pauline Ralph – West Hoathly WI)

Snow piled high on the beach at Elmer in January 1963. This was a winter to rival that bitter one of 1947, with the sea itself freezing in places and snow that lay for months into the spring. (Heather Crate – Hunston WI)

The new Chichester Festival Theatre in 1962. It has developed into a major artistic venue, both locally and nationally. (Betty Pennicott – Hunston WI)

THE SIXTIES AND SEVENTIES (1960–1979)

Cars were becoming part of the family by 1961, when this Morris Ten was about on the roads.
(Betty Pennicott – Hunston WI)

A sign of the times – cars parked outside cottages at Barleycroft, Albourne in 1965.
(Albourne WI)

The 'Old Crocks' veteran cars race from London to Brighton in 1965. Many of those 'modern' cars that passed them on the road that day have since become veterans in their own right! (Albourne WI)

Children at Albourne primary school in 1965. Schools, and methods of teaching, were beginning to change, perhaps not wholly for the better, but these children would have greater opportunities than their parents or grandparents could have dreamed of. (Albourne WI)

Shipley Windmill under restoration in 1969, and complete in 1970. A greater appreciation of such once workaday buildings has thankfully saved some of the last of their kind.
(Betty Pennicott – Hunston WI)

Ardingly Reservoir was constructed during the very dry summer of 1976 by Mid Sussex Water Company, by building a dam to collect water from Shell Brook and Ardingly Brook at Wakehurst where they converge before joining the Ouse. It was expected to take two years to fill, but the following winter was so wet that it filled in a few months. It covered a beautiful valley and a very old timber-framed farmhouse was lost, but it has been well landscaped and is today an attractive feature.
(Rosemary Hodgson – Ardingly WI)

THE SIXTIES AND SEVENTIES (1960–1979)

The prizewinners in the East Dean 'Best Decorated Cottage' competition for the Queen's Silver Jubilee celebrations in 1977. All over the county, street parties, sports, dances and bonfires marked the occasion.
(Singleton & East Dean WI)

Opposite St Leonard's (South Stoke) Christmas bazaar in the late 1970s, held at the Red Cross centre, Arundel. How many bazaars today would be selling unskinned rabbits and sacks of potatoes?
(Rose Stacey – Arundel Green Lane WI)

Another recreational amenity was created by allowing rock climbing on the St Hill Rocks, near East Grinstead, by Weirwood Reservoir, shown here in 1973.
(Sheila Wells – Burgess Hill WI)

MODERN TIMES

(After 1980)

As the end of the century approaches, West Sussex is still one of the most wooded counties in England, with Areas of Outstanding Natural Beauty in the Downs, the Weald and Chichester Harbour. The county has over 2,500 miles of footpaths, the best known being the long distance path, the South Downs Way, which runs from Eastbourne to Winchester.

The two main rivers are the Arun, entering the sea at Littlehampton, and the Ouse at Shoreham. Shoreham Harbour handles three million tonnes of goods each year, and Littlehampton about 300,000 tonnes. It is still a maritime county, and the sea provides both work and leisure activities.

Goodwood, the family seat of the Duke of Richmond & Gordon, boasts a fine racecourse which comes into its own during the last week of July – Glorious Goodwood. Motor racing ceased on the estate in the 1960s, when it was felt the high speed that cars could now attain might be dangerous for spectators, and the track became an airfield for light aircraft. It is hoped to restore motor racing there on a limited scale in the future.

While supermarkets took their hold on our shopping habits in the 1960s, hypermarkets and shopping malls were the concepts of the Eighties and early Nineties. They often took the heart out of traditional town centres. Small shops have struggled to survive. There are signs that the struggle has had its effect, and people are beginning to appreciate the benefits of the corner shop once again. Initiatives to revitalise our towns, and support village shops and post offices, will hopefully stop the decline.

Village life has changed immensely since the beginning of the century. When new methods of farming reduced the need for manpower on the land, an exodus from the villages began. Cottages were bought by people who commuted to work, or had retired. Schools closed for lack of children, and shops for lack of customers. A car became essential as rural bus services and train services declined. Yet there is a continuing buoyancy in community life, and a willingness to work together to support local amenities, that bodes well for the future.

On the land farmers have had to look at new ways to make a living. Some have done so by renovating old farm buildings for sale or holiday lets, or by leasing them out to small businesses. 'Pick Your Own' for fruit and vegetables has also proved a popular diversification.

Attitudes to animals have changed over the century. Shoreham suffered ugly scenes when people protested against the export of live animals to the Continent.

The Great Storm swept across southern England in 1987 and caused a huge amount of damage within West Sussex. Thankfully, there was no loss of life but roofs were lifted off buildings, walls knocked down, caravans turned over and ships blown onto the coast. Power lines came down, and an estimated three million trees were destroyed. Some homes were without electricity for days and gangs of workmen had to be brought in from other areas to cope with restoring power.

After 1980

There was another calamity when a disastrous fire engulfed the National Trust property of Uppark. Years of painstaking work have finally restored the building to its full glory.

Great interest is shown in the life we lived 'in the old days'. Sussex's industrial past is commemorated at the Amberley Chalk Pits Museum, which was a working chalk pit until the 1960s. A past of a different kind came under the spotlight when Boxgrove Man was discovered in a disused sand pit.

In the early 1990s the various 50th anniversaries of the events of the Second World War were commemorated by several events, including D-Day street parties and celebrations. Tangmere airfield, which played such an important part in the Battle of Britain, now houses a Military Aircraft Museum.

Looking back to old times – Audrey Broad relived the days of the land girls at the Weald & Downland Open Air Museum's Women's Land Army and Timber Corps Exhibition in October 1994.

(Audrey Broad – Southwater Weald WI)

MODERN TIMES (AFTER 1980)

THEN & NOW. The crossroads in Fernhurst in the 1920s, 1940s and today. Road markings, pavements and street lights are the main alterations to be seen. (Helen Ollin – Fernhurst WI)

ASLEMERE ROAD, FERNHURST

*A timeless scene – All
Saints' church, Lindfield in
the snow, 1991.
(Jean Parmenter –
Lindfield WI)*

MODERN TIMES (AFTER 1980)

THEN & NOW. Kirdford village shop in 1900, with buckets hanging on the railings outside and ewer and basin sets to be seen amongst the goods in the window. Today it is Chestnut House, a private residence.
(Mavis Thompson – Kirdford WI)

Canning fruit and vegetables was started by the Women's Institutes during the Second World War, and at Fittleworth it continued until the 1980s. After sterilisation the cans were tied securely into metal containers and lowered into the millstream for cooling.
(Fittleworth WI)

THEN & NOW. How the traffic has increased! Horsham Road, Handcross in 1907 and in 1996, when an accident on the A23 caused huge tailbacks.
(Gladys Toogood – Handcross WI)

A smith attracting attention at the Crawley High Street Festival street fair – the first of the annual Crawley festivals in 1986.
(Jean Morgan – Crawley WI)

Riding up Viaduct Hill at Balcombe in 1994 with the drag hunt.
(Paula Bateman – Balcombe WI)

The London to Brighton bike race passes through Sussex on the third Sunday in June, in aid of charity. It started as an event in 1975 and often causes chaos while it lasts! Local Scouts usually provide a 'food stop' for participants.
(Rosemary Hodgson – Ardingly WI)

One of the casualties of the hurricane that swept across southern England in October 1987. This building belonging to the West Sussex County Council School & Grounds Maintenance Dept at Chichester was totally destroyed by the winds. (Irene Newbold – Hunston WI)

Roads all over the county were blocked by fallen trees and power lines in October 1987, and when they were once more reopened it was as desolate avenues of sawn trunks and roots, as here at Oldlands Avenue, Balcombe. (Balcombe WI)

93

MODERN TIMES (AFTER 1980)

THEN & NOW. An early bus on the A27 at The Swan, Bosham in the 1920s. Today a similar bus is an attraction at the Amberley Chalk Pits Museum.
(Joyce Stant – East Wittering WI; Anne Duffy – Hunston WI)

In 1994 the river Lavant became a raging torrent due to the high water table, and flooded the Hornet area of Chichester. The Fire Service were unable to cope alone so army Green Goddesses were brought out of retirement to help. Water was pumped by means of hoses to the Chichester canal basin some three quarters of a mile away. Plans were even made to evacuate residents in the south of the city if the situation deteriorated further, but fortunately this did not happen.
(Betty Pennicott – Hunston WI)

THEN & NOW. Looking towards the pier at Bognor. The early view was after 1912, when the foreshore and was built at a cost of over £20,000 by Mr Carter and Mr Shanly. Things have changed – the beach in the early postcard (right) is depicted as soft golden sand. (Sylvia Endacott; Betty Pennicott – Hunston WI)

Above Terrorism came to Bognor with an IRA bomb in August 1994. Afterwards the police appealed for information. (Sylvia Endacott)

Inland waterways are now used for leisure. This flotilla on the Chichester Canal was marking the Golden Jubilee of the Inland Waterway. (Anne Duffy – Hunston WI)

For the VE Day 50th anniversary celebrations in 1995, this table at Ardingly stretched 100 yards along the road. Street parties proved a way of bringing communities together for this commemoration. (Rosemary Hodgson – Ardingly WI)